# Video AI from NVIDIA

# A New Digital Frontier

Taylor Royce

# DEDICATION

This book is dedicated to all individuals who dare to see the future and work toward molding it.

This work is dedicated to the visionaries and innovators who push the frontiers of what is possible and whose unwavering curiosity propels technological advancements.

Your enthusiasm and commitment are the source of motivation for these pages, experts, enthusiasts, and students who want to learn about and use AI.

And this book is dedicated with sincere gratitude to my family and friends, whose steadfast belief and support have been a continual source of strength and drive.

I hope that this exploration of AI and video material will spark original thought, encourage artistic expression, and pave the way for a time when technology improves both our quality of life and our comprehension of the outside world.

# CONTENTS

# ACKNOWLEDGMENTS

This book is the result of a team effort, with numerous people and organizations lending their support and contributions to make it a reality.

The author expresses sincere gratitude to all individuals who offered insightful analysis, insightful research, and insightful comments that greatly influenced the direction and content of this work. Your knowledge and commitment have been invaluable.

I also want to express my gratitude to the publishing team for their dedication and expertise. Their help has been effective and encouraging in turning this work into a book that has been published.

To my peers and colleagues: Your thought-provoking conversations and attitude of cooperation have greatly enhanced our effort. Your suggestions have been an inspiration and have contributed to the content's richness and relevance.

I am also appreciative of my friends and family for their constant encouragement and support. Your perseverance and faith in this endeavor have served as a continuous source of inspiration.

I would like to conclude by thanking the readers for their interest in this work. With any luck, the information and understanding I've shared here will help you further explore the exciting world of artificial intelligence and video production.

We are grateful to everyone who has participated in this adventure.

## DISCLAIMER

This book contains opinions and information that are meant mainly for general informative purposes; it is not professional or expert advice. The author and publisher do not guarantee the correctness, reliability, or completeness of the material presented herein, even though every effort has been taken to assure its accuracy and completeness.

The opinions and understanding of the author as of the book's publishing date are reflected in its content. When making decisions based on the information supplied, readers should use their own discretion and seek advice from qualified professionals. Any errors or omissions in this book's content, as well as any repercussions resulting from using it, are not the responsibility of the author or publisher.

The mention of certain businesses, technologies, or goods does not imply approval or recommendation. No products or technology mentioned are guaranteed to be effective, safe, or perform as described by the author or publisher.

It is recommended that readers look for supplementary materials and professional viewpoints to enhance the information provided. The content in this book may become out of date or susceptible to change due to the rapidly changing nature of industry standards and technology.

# CHAPTER 1

## 1.1: NVIDIA Makes a Move in the Video AI Space

### NVIDIA's Position in the Technology Sector

Known for creating cutting-edge graphics processing units (GPUs) that transformed the gaming industry, NVIDIA has a long history of being a leader in the technology business. NVIDIA's technology is not limited to gaming; it is also used in data centers, the automotive industry, and artificial intelligence (AI). By continuously pushing the envelope of what is conceivable, the company's innovations have solidified its leadership in the tech sector.

### The Company's AI and Machine Learning Priorities

NVIDIA has increased its attention to AI and machine learning in recent years after realizing these technologies

1

have the ability to revolutionize a wide range of sectors. NVIDIA has made it possible for researchers and developers to create sophisticated AI models that can solve challenging challenges by creating potent GPUs and AI frameworks like CUDA. This deliberate focus has put NVIDIA in the vanguard of the AI revolution, propelling developments in fields like video content, autonomous cars, and natural language processing.

## Declaration of an Upcoming AI Model for Video Content

An important first step has been taken with NVIDIA's entry into video AI. The business just revealed that it has created an innovative AI model especially for video content. This model utilizes deep learning algorithms and NVIDIA's cutting-edge GPU technology to accomplish a variety of tasks that were previously believed to be the domain of human competence. The news has created a lot of excitement in the computer world and highlighted NVIDIA's dedication to breaking new ground in artificial intelligence.

## 1.2: NVIDIA's Video AI's Possible Uses

## Video Retouching and Editing

Video editing and enhancement represent one of the most exciting use cases for NVIDIA's video AI technology. The editing process can be greatly accelerated by the AI model's ability to automate laborious operations like stabilization, noise reduction, and color correction. It can also improve visual clarity and upscaling of lower resolution content, which makes it easier for content makers to create high-quality videos with less work.

## Creating and Synthesizing Videos

Additionally, visual synthesis and creation could be completely transformed by NVIDIA's video AI. The AI can generate missing frames in already-existing film or produce realistic video material from scratch using sophisticated generative techniques. This feature can be very helpful in the film industry since it can be used to generate whole new sequences or bridge gaps in existing ones, saving money on expensive special effects and

3

reshoots.

## Analysis and Interpretation of Videos

The analysis and comprehension of videos is a crucial use case for NVIDIA's video AI. With the help of AI, video information can be automatically analyzed to identify scenes, objects, and activities. This results in useful metadata that can be utilized for a variety of applications. It can be used, for example, in content moderation to flag offensive content, in sports analytics to track player movements, and in security systems to detect suspicious actions. This degree of comprehension makes it possible to manage video content more effectively and efficiently.

## Video Lookup and Suggestion

The video search and recommendation systems are improved by the AI model's capacity to comprehend and evaluate video information. The AI can increase the precision of search results by producing thorough metadata, assisting users in locating particular scenes or subjects within a sizable video archive. Furthermore, recommendation algorithms powered by it can make appropriate content suggestions based on user viewing history and preferences, improving the entire YouTube and Netflix experience.

## 1.3: Competition and Industry Impact

### Analyses for the Video Content Sector

The video content sector is expected to experience significant changes following the launch of NVIDIA's video AI. It can save production costs and boost productivity by automating labor-intensive operations, allowing content producers to produce more work more quickly. This technological development has the potential to democratize the video production industry by providing a wider variety of creators from indie filmmakers to major studios with access to high-caliber tools.

### Potential Upheaval of Conventional Video Processes

The video AI from NVIDIA has the potential to drastically alter current video workflows. AI is now capable of performing tasks that formerly required expert human interaction, which may decrease the need for some positions in the sector. Professionals can, however, take advantage of this disruption to advance and concentrate on more strategic and creative facets of video creation, using AI as a potent tool rather than as a replacement.

## Comparison of Video AI Initiatives by Other Tech Giants

Several tech behemoths are involved in the video AI market, and they are all vying for the top spot by developing new technologies. Significant progress has also been made in the development of AI models for video content by businesses such as Google, Facebook, and Amazon. Facebook concentrates on augmented reality experiences and video content regulation, while Google employs its AI powers for YouTube to improve ad targeting and content discovery. Developers may get AI-powered video analysis services from Amazon through AWS. The fact that NVIDIA has entered this competitive market shows how quickly innovation is happening and how important it is to steer the direction of video content in the future.

## 1.4: Public View and Expectations

## First Reaction of the Public to the News

The general public's initial response to NVIDIA's announcement has been a mixture of interest and excitement. NVIDIA has received high marks from industry insiders and tech enthusiasts for its ongoing innovation and AI leadership. The idea of AI-powered video tools has attracted a lot of interest, and many people are excited about the model's impending release and possible uses in a variety of industries.

## Customers' Excitement and Concerns

Concerns as well as joy have been voiced by customers about the new AI model. On the one hand, the prospect of improved video quality, more tailored content suggestions, and cutting-edge tools for creating videos is very alluring. However, there are also worries about the ethical ramifications of AI-generated material, privacy concerns associated with video analysis, and the possibility of job losses brought on by automation. These conflicting responses emphasize the necessity of open communication and the prudent application of AI technology.

## Potential Gains and Losses for Audience Members

The advantages of NVIDIA's video AI for viewers are significant. The viewing experience can be greatly enhanced by improved video quality and tailored recommendations, which will make it simpler to find and consume material. Still, there can be disadvantages to take into account. There are concerns over the validity of content and the possibility of abuse due to the extensive usage of AI in video production and analysis. In order to allay these worries and preserve audience confidence, it will be imperative to make sure AI technologies are applied morally and openly.

NVIDIA's foray into the video AI space is a noteworthy advancement in the technology sector, with the potential to revolutionize the production, evaluation, and consumption of video content. Like any technical innovation, it presents opportunities as well as obstacles, therefore in order to optimize its advantages and reduce its hazards, it must be used responsibly and with careful thought.

# CHAPTER 2

## NVIDIA's Video AI's Technical Foundations

## 2.1: Fundamental Algorithms and Technologies

### Neural Networks and Deep Learning

NVIDIA's video AI engine is based on deep learning, which is a subset of machine learning. It entails teaching multi-layered artificial neural networks to identify patterns and make judgments using a lot of data. Because these networks are made to resemble the way the human brain processes information, they have the capacity to learn and develop over time.

- **CNNs, or convolutional neural networks:** CNNs are often employed in image and video analysis, and they are particularly good at spotting spatial hierarchies in visual data. They work very well at identifying persons, objects, and actions in video frames.

- **RNNs (Recurrent Neural Networks):** RNNs are used to analyze temporal dynamics in movies, which includes recognizing the order of actions or forecasting future frames. They are useful for sequence prediction and temporal data analysis.

## Image Processing and Computer Vision Techniques

Video AI relies heavily on computer vision, which gives machines the ability to comprehend and decide based on visual inputs. NVIDIA's video AI processes and analyzes video footage by utilizing cutting-edge computer vision techniques.

- **Segmentation of Images:** To make analysis easier, this technique includes segmenting an image. It aids with the recognition and isolation of various items inside each frame for video AI.
- **Identifying Objects:** Object identification techniques improve the AI's comprehension and interaction capabilities with visual content by identifying and categorizing items within video

frames.

- **Flow of Optics:** This method helps with action detection and video stabilization by tracking object motion between successive frames.

## Natural Language Understanding for Videos

In video AI, natural language processing (NLP) is essential, especially for tasks like content recommendation, video annotation, and summarization.

- **Automatic Speech Recognition (ASR):** Transforms spoken words in films into text so that artificial intelligence (AI) can comprehend and interpret conversation.
- **Text Summarization:** Produces brief synopsis or summaries of video footage to facilitate indexing and searching.
- **Sentiment Analysis:** Evaluates the emotional content of speech and text in videos, offering more in-depth understanding of audience responses and the significance of the information.

## 2.2: Training Procedure and Data Requirements

## Huge Datasets for Training Models

Large volumes of data are needed to train an AI model for video material in order to guarantee accuracy and resilience. Massive datasets containing a variety of video formats, such as TV series, movies, user-generated material, and security footage, are used to train NVIDIA's video artificial intelligence system.

- **Diversity of Data:** A broad range of scenarios, lighting settings, and video qualities must be covered in the training data in order to create a versatile AI.
- **Annotation and Labeling:** To give the AI thorough training examples, every video segment must be painstakingly annotated with pertinent labels, such as object categories, actions, and scene descriptions.

## Difficulties in Privacy and Data Curation

There are many obstacles in the way of curating the datasets required for training, especially when it comes to data protection and quality.

- **Data Quality:** To create a dependable AI model, it is essential to make sure that the training data is clear, varied, and indicative of actual situations.
- **Protective Issues:** Ethical and legal concerns arise when using video data, particularly from personal content or surveillance film. Sensitive data must be anonymized, and appropriate consent must be obtained before using the information for training.

## Ethical Factors in Data Utilization

When creating and using video AI technology, ethical issues are crucial.

- **Bias Mitigation:** Consistently observing the model's performance and paying close attention to the diversity of the training data are necessary to guarantee that the AI model is impartial and equitable.
- **Transparency:** Upholding openness regarding the use of data and AI decision-making procedures

fosters confidence among stakeholders and users.

- **Accountability:** Setting up procedures for accountability and taking care of any possible abuse or damage brought about by AI is essential for its ethical application.

## 2.3: Acceleration and Optimization of Hardware

## GPU Advantage of NVIDIA for AI Tasks

Because of their legendary capacity for parallel processing, NVIDIA GPUs are the perfect choice for managing the computational needs of deep learning and artificial intelligence applications.

**CUDA Platform:** With NVIDIA's CUDA platform, developers can leverage GPU capability for AI and machine learning applications, resulting in notable speed gains over CPU-based processing.

**Tensor Cores:** With the purpose of speeding up deep learning computations, these specialized cores allow for quicker neural network training and inference.

## Video Processing Hardware with Specialization

Apart from general-purpose GPUs, NVIDIA creates hardware specifically designed for activities related to video processing.

- **NVIDIA DGX Systems:** With high-performance processing power and storage to manage massive video collections, these systems are tailored for AI research and development.
- **Platforms Jetson:** NVIDIA's Jetson platforms, aimed at edge computing applications, offer strong AI capabilities in a small form size, appropriate for real-time video processing and analysis.

## Methods of Optimization for Real-Time Performance

For many video AI applications, like interactive content and live video streaming, real-time speed is crucial.

**Model Pruning:** Cutting superfluous parameters from the neural network can reduce its size and speed up processing without sacrificing accuracy too much.

**Quantization:** Reducing the computational load and speeding up inference can be achieved by converting the model weights and activations from floating-point to lower-precision forms, such as 8-bit integers.

**Pipeline Optimization:** By effectively controlling the data flow and processing pipeline, latency is reduced and video frames are processed quickly and smoothly.

## 2.4: Prospective Advancements and Restraints

### Research on Video AI Advances

The field of video artificial intelligence is advancing significantly thanks to ongoing research and development, which is expanding the potential applications of AI in video content.

- **Enhanced Accuracy:** Video synthesis, object detection, and action recognition are becoming more accurate thanks to improved algorithms and more datasets.

- **Transfer Learning:** By utilizing pre-trained models on sizable datasets, training on particular video tasks can be completed more quickly and effectively, increasing performance and requiring fewer resources.

## Anticipated NVIDIA Model Capabilities

A number of state-of-the-art features that could revolutionize the production and consumption of video content are anticipated from NVIDIA's video AI model.

- **Automated Editing:** The video creation process can be streamlined by the AI's ability to independently complete complicated editing tasks including scene transitions, background removal, and effects application.
- **Enhanced Personalization:** The AI may provide highly personalized content recommendations and customized viewing experiences by analyzing viewer preferences and habits.
- **Real-Time Analysis:** The AI can enable applications like live event coverage, security monitoring, and interactive entertainment by processing and analyzing video footage in real-time.

## Technological Obstacles and Difficulties

To fully fulfill the potential of video artificial intelligence, a number of technological obstacles and problems must be overcome, despite the encouraging improvements.

- **Scalability:** A major obstacle still lies in ensuring that the AI model can scale effectively to manage enormous volumes of video data and a variety of use cases.

- **Interpretability:** Gaining users' trust and adoption of the AI depends on making its decision-making procedures clear and intelligible to them.

- **Ethical and Legal Concerns:** Regulation and continual attention are needed to address concerns about bias, data privacy, and the possible exploitation of AI-generated content.

The sophisticated deep learning methods, significant data needs, and potent hardware acceleration forms the foundation of NVIDIA's video artificial intelligence. Despite the wide range of possible uses and capabilities, the appropriate development and implementation of this revolutionary technology depend heavily on giving ethical and practical issues due attention.

# CHAPTER 3

## LEGAL IMPLICATIONS AND COPYRIGHT

## 3.1: Concerns About Copyright Violations

### Training using Copyrighted Content

There are serious ethical and legal issues when AI models are trained with copyrighted content. Large amounts of data, some of which might be covered by copyright rules, are frequently fed into the AI during the process.

- **Area of Application:** Without express consent from the owners of the content, training AI models on copyrighted video material may be illegal.
- **Secondary Works:** Content produced by the AI that is based on or closely resembles copyrighted material could be categorized as a derivative work, which could provide legal issues.

# Litigation Threats from Content Owners

Owners of intellectual property have a strong incentive to safeguard it, and if they feel their rights have been violated, they may take legal action.

- **Cease and Desist Orders:** To stop additional usage of their copyrighted work, content owners may issue cease and desist orders.
- **Legal actions:** In more extreme situations, content creators can sue for money damages or an injunction to prevent their work from being used in AI training.
- **Consultations and Agreements:** It is possible for businesses such as NVIDIA to negotiate settlements or license agreements with content owners in order to use the copyrighted information.

# Legal Defenses and Fair Use

According to a legal theory known as fair use, certain restricted uses of copyrighted content are allowed without the owners' consent.

- **Transformative Use:** If the AI uses the copyrighted content in a way that adds fresh expression or meaning, then such use can be considered fair use.

- Purpose and Character: Fair use is also determined in part by the purpose and character of the usage, including whether it is for commercial or educational purposes.

- **Amount and Substantiality:** When assessing claims of fair use, consideration is given to the quantity and significance of the copyrighted material used.

## 3.2: Misinformation and Deepfakes

## Implications for Ethics in AI-Generated Video Content

Deepfakes and other AI-generated video content present serious ethical issues.

- **Manipulation and Deception:** Realistic but fraudulent videos made with deepfakes have the potential to mislead viewers and sway public opinion.

- **Loss of Trust:** People may find it more difficult to discern between real and false videos as a result of the prevalence of deepfakes.

## Risk of Abuse and Misuse

When AI-generated video content is misused, there can be detrimental effects on both society and the individual.

- **Political Manipulation:** Deepfakes are a tool that may be used to propagate false information, sway elections, and wreck reputations.
- **Privacy Violations:** Deepfake films of people that are produced and shared without their permission may violate their privacy and cause them mental pain.

## Accountability and Regulation Measures

Robust regulation and accountability measures are crucial to reducing the hazards connected with deepfakes and misinformation.

- **Legal Frameworks:** To address the production and propagation of deepfakes, governments and regulatory organizations are creating legal frameworks.

- **Technological Solutions:** Organizations such as NVIDIA are making investments in technology designed to identify and stop the improper usage of content generated by AI.

- **Transparency and Disclosure:** Maintaining accountability and trust can be facilitated by establishing explicit disclosure standards and ensuring transparency regarding AI-generated content.

## 3.3: Protection of Intellectual Property

**Shielding AI Technology at NVIDIA**

To keep a competitive edge and promote innovation, AI technology intellectual property (IP) must be protected.

- **Trade Secrets:** To avoid unwanted access and usage, proprietary data, techniques, and procedures can be protected as trade secrets.

- **Nondisclosure Agreements:** Confidentiality agreements between partners and workers aid in safeguarding unique technology and sensitive data.

## Strategies for Copyright and Patents

AI innovations can be legally protected through the strategic application of copyrights and patents.

- **Patents:** Securing a patent for novel AI techniques and technology may grant the exclusive right to employ and market them.
- **Released under license**: Original works of authorship, including code, documentation, and datasets utilized in AI development, may be covered by copyright protection.

## Partnerships and Licenses

Partnerships and licensing arrangements can support the commercialization and wider application of AI technologies while preserving intellectual property rights.

- **Licensing Agreements:** Permitting the use of copyrighted works or patented technologies can lead to cash generation and foster collaboration.
- **Partnerships:** Creating strategic alliances with other businesses and academic organizations can spur creativity and increase the application of AI technologies.

## 3.4: Future Regulations and the Legal Environment

## Extant Intellectual Property and Copyright Laws

The current IP and copyright rules offer a framework for safeguarding inventions and creative works.

- **Copyright Act:** Authors of creative works of literature, music, and film are protected by the Copyright Act.
- **Patent Act:** The Patent Act encourages creativity and investment in emerging technologies by granting inventors the exclusive right to their ideas.

# Developing AI Legal Frameworks

New legal frameworks are developing in response to the particular consequences and issues posed by AI technology as it advances.

- **AI-Specific Legislation:** To control the advancement and application of AI technologies, certain jurisdictions are creating laws specifically pertaining to AI.
- **Ethical Guidelines:** Industry associations and international organizations are developing moral standards for the appropriate application of artificial intelligence.

## Probable Modifications to the Regulatory Framework

As technology develops and the effects on society become more obvious, the regulatory landscape surrounding AI is probably going to change more.

- **Increased Oversight:** To guarantee the moral and responsible application of AI, governments may impose more regulations and oversight.

- **International Cooperation:** Addressing cross-border issues and encouraging the proper use of AI technologies can be accomplished through international cooperation and harmonization of AI rules.

NVIDIA's video AI technology has intricate and wide-ranging copyright and legal ramifications. A comprehensive strategy involving legal tactics, moral considerations, and strong regulatory structures is needed to address these issues. Through careful navigation of these obstacles, NVIDIA can fully utilize the promise of its artificial intelligence technologies, all the while maintaining legal compliance and building public confidence.

# CHAPTER 4

## 4.1: Dangers to Data Privacy

## Acquiring and Preserving User Information

AI systems' gathering and storing of user data poses serious privacy concerns that must be carefully managed.

- **Data Volume and Sensitivity:** AI systems gather enormous volumes of delicate personal data, particularly when handling video footage. This contains behavioral patterns, location data, and facial recognition data.

- **Storage Issues:** It's critical to store this data safely. Inadequate security protocols may result in unwanted entry and possible data breaches.

## Applications for Data Misuse and Breach

AI-driven video systems raise serious concerns about the possibility of data breaches and exploitation.

- **Cyberattacks**: Because AI systems store important data, they are easy targets for cyberattacks. Data about users may be stolen, altered, or held ransom by hackers.
- **Data Misuse:** Even with strong security, there is a chance that data will be misused either internally or by other parties resulting in invasions of users' privacy and possible injury.

## Regulations Concerning User Consent and Data Protection

Sustaining trust and legal compliance requires user consent and compliance with data protection laws.

- **Informed Consent:** It is essential to have users' express, informed consent before collecting and using their data. Customers should be given the choice to opt out and be informed about how their data will be used.

- **Accordance with Rules:** Businesses have to abide by applicable laws and data protection standards like the CCPA and GDPR. To safeguard user privacy, these policies impose strict guidelines on data collection, storage, and processing.

## 4.2: Privacy and Surveillance Issues

## The Function of AI in Video Surveillance

Artificial intelligence (AI) technologies have a big impact on video surveillance capabilities, which raises serious privacy issues.

- **Advanced Surveillance Capabilities:** AI can improve video surveillance by offering cutting-edge functions including real-time monitoring, behavior analysis, and facial recognition. Although these features can increase security, there are serious privacy concerns as well.
- **Surveillance's Pervasiveness:** The ongoing monitoring of public and private locations that could

result from the widespread use of AI-powered surveillance systems could have an adverse effect on people's privacy.

## Affect on Personal Privacy

AI surveillance has significant effects on people's right to privacy.

- **Erosion of Privacy:** Constant data collecting and monitoring can weaken people's feelings of privacy, making them feel like they're being watched and examined all the time.
- **Chilling Effect:** People may become less inclined to express themselves openly or participate in particular activities as a result of the existence of surveillance technologies.

## Security and Civil Liberties in Balance

It might be difficult to strike the correct balance between the demands of security and civil liberties.

- **Security Benefits:** AI-powered monitoring can improve criminal prevention, public safety, and investigative support.

- **Legal Rights:** Ensuring that monitoring devices are not utilized for discriminatory purposes or unjustified breaches of privacy is crucial in safeguarding human liberties.

- **Policy Structures:** Creating precise policy guidelines and oversight procedures can aid in striking a balance between the requirement for security and the defense of people's right to privacy.

## 4.3: Protection and Anonymization of Data

### Methods for Protecting User Information

Ensuring user privacy requires the use of effective data anonymization and protection measures.

- **Anonymization:** Data sets can be made more private by removing or encrypting personally identifiable information. One can use methods like tokenization, differential privacy, and data masking.

- **Appropriate Name:** Pseudonyms can be used to replace identifiable information, lowering privacy hazards and enabling data analysis.

## Technologies Improving Privacy

Using privacy-enhancing technologies (PETs) can help to safeguard user information even further.

- **Encryption:** Data that is encrypted both in transit and at rest is protected against access by unauthorized parties.
- **Secure Multi-Party Computation:** This enables cooperation on data analysis between parties without disclosing any private information to one another.
- **Federated Learning:** This method maintains localized and secure data while allowing AI models to be trained across numerous decentralized devices.

## Data Handling Industry Best Practices

Maintaining security and privacy in data processing requires adherence to industry best practices.

- **Data Minimization:** Reducing the risk of privacy breaches is achieved by collecting only the data required for particular objectives.

- **Access Controls:** Unauthorized access can be avoided by putting strong access controls in place and making sure that only authorized workers have access to sensitive data.

- **Regular Audits:** Finding and addressing such vulnerabilities is facilitated by conducting routine audits and evaluations of data protection procedures.

## 4.4: Responsible AI and Ethical Principles

### Creating AI Ethical Frameworks

Responsible AI use requires the establishment of strong ethical frameworks for AI development and use.

- **Ethical Principles:** Fairness, accountability, and openness are a few examples of ethical principles that should guide the development and application of AI systems.

- **Inclusive Design:** It is crucial to make sure AI systems are inclusively developed and do not reinforce prejudice or discrimination.

## Accountability and Transparency in AI Systems

The development of trust in AI technologies is contingent upon transparency and accountability.

- **Explainability:** AI systems ought to be transparent and able to clearly articulate the reasoning behind their judgments. This enhances users' comprehension and confidence in the technology.
- **Methods of Accountability:** It is essential to set up procedures for holding users and developers responsible for the moral use of AI systems. Legal structures, supervisory organizations, and explicit guidelines are examples of this.

## Establishing User Trust

Developing and preserving user trust is essential to AI technology adoption success.

- **User Engagement:** Including user input in AI development procedures and keeping users informed might help build confidence.
- **Clear Communication:** User concerns can be reduced by offering clear and transparent information about the data that is gathered, how it is used, and how AI systems operate.
- **Ethical Commitments:** Long-term user trust can be developed by exhibiting a dedication to data protection and ethical behavior.

It is critical that privacy and data security issues are taken into consideration when developing and implementing AI technology. Companies such as NVIDIA can enhance confidence and guarantee the appropriate application of artificial intelligence in video content by putting strong data protection measures in place, striking a balance between surveillance and civil freedoms, and abiding by ethical norms.

# CHAPTER 5

## BUSINESS OPPORTUNITIES AND ECONOMIC IMPACT

## 5.1: Video AI's Market Potential

## Industries Using Video AI to Their Advantage

Video AI has a huge market potential, and its integration might have a major positive impact on several industrial verticals.

- **Media and Entertainment:** Video AI can transform the production process, improving efficiency and quality while revolutionizing content creation, editing, and distribution. Applications include the creation of special effects, automated video editing, and tailored content recommendations.
- **Healthcare:** By analyzing medical imagery and videos, video AI can help with medical diagnostics, enhancing patient outcomes and diagnostic accuracy.

- **Retail and E-commerce:** Virtual try-ons, tailored purchasing suggestions, and enhanced security via cutting-edge monitoring are just a few ways that AI-driven video analytics may improve the consumer experience.

- **Security and Surveillance:** Video AI gives security systems stronger security measures by enhancing them with real-time threat identification, anomaly detection, and facial recognition.

- **Education and E-learning:** Video AI can support the production of instructional content, automated grading of video assignments, and personalized, interactive learning experiences.

## NVIDIA's Revenue Generation Models

To take advantage of the market potential for video AI, NVIDIA can investigate several income generation strategies.

- **Licensing AI Models**: Granting licenses to other businesses for AI models and technology can generate a consistent flow of income. This covers licenses for particular uses, including surveillance or video editing.

- **Subscription Services:** You can draw in a diverse clientele by providing AI-powered services like cloud-based video processing and analytics on a subscription basis.

- **Custom Solutions:** Creating custom AI solutions that meet the demands of big businesses can lead to premium pricing and long-term relationships.

- **Collaborations and Partnerships:** Forming strategic alliances with other prominent figures in the sector might result in joint development of artificial intelligence solutions, revenue sharing, and market expansion.

## Demand for Jobs and Economic Growth

The development of video AI has the potential to boost the economy and generate new employment possibilities in a number of industries.

- **Innovation and firms:** As video AI develops, it will probably inspire new ideas that will result in the formation of firms devoted to creating AI-powered video solutions.

- **Job Creation:** Automation may eliminate certain employment, but it will also generate new positions in data science, AI system maintenance, AI development, and other fields that use AI technologies.

- **Development of Skills:** The need for individuals with expertise in AI and video technologies will push academic institutions to create new training programs and curriculum, which will boost the economy even more.

## 5.2: Traditional Industries Are Being Disrupted

### Effect on Entertainment and Media

Video AI is going to cause a major upheaval in the media and entertainment sector.

- **Content development:** Artificial intelligence (AI) can save production time and costs by automating repetitive operations in content development, such as scene composition, video editing, and CGI rendering.

- **customization:** AI-powered customization can provide viewers with material that is specifically tailored to them, increasing satisfaction and engagement.

- **Enhanced Viewing Experiences:** Cutting-edge methods for video processing and enhancement can bring new interactive elements and improve video quality, completely changing the way that information is seen.

## Modifications to Marketing and Advertising

Video Artificial Intelligence will bring about big changes to the advertising and marketing industry.

- **tailored Advertising:** AI is able to deliver highly tailored ads by analyzing viewer behavior and preferences, which boosts ad effectiveness and return on investment.

- **material Customization:** By utilizing AI, marketers may provide tailored advertising material for various audience segments, increasing relevance and interaction.

- **Real-time Analytics:** With the use of AI-powered analytics, marketers can make dynamic adjustments to their campaigns by getting real-time insights about the effectiveness of their ads.

## Modifications to Content Development and Distribution

The creation and distribution of content across multiple platforms will be revolutionized by video AI.

- **Automated Content Creation**: AI can improve pre existing footage or create brand-new video content from scratch, creating new avenues for artistic expression.
- **Efficient dissemination:** By anticipating viewer preferences and suggesting the ideal platforms and release periods, AI can optimize the dissemination of content.
- **Monetization techniques:** Based on viewer behavior and market trends, AI may assist content creators and distributors in creating creative

monetization techniques, like dynamic pricing and subscription models.

## 5.3: Joint Ventures and Partnerships

## Crucial Partnerships with Sector Leaders

The integration and acceptance of video AI can be accelerated by forming strategic collaborations with important industry players.

- **Tech Companies:** Sharing technical know-how and co-developing cutting-edge AI solutions are two benefits of collaborating with other tech companies.
- **Media Corporations:** Collaborations with media corporations can promote the use of AI technology in the creation and dissemination of content, resulting in gains for both parties.
- **Medical Service Providers:** Working together with healthcare professionals can increase the application of AI in patient care and medical diagnostics, enhancing both operational effectiveness and health outcomes.

## Development of Ecosystems for Video AI

The creation of a strong ecosystem is essential to the success and broad acceptance of video AI.

- **Open Platforms:** Establishing open AI platforms can encourage creativity and community involvement by enabling developers to create and implement their own video AI applications.
- **Standardization:** By establishing industry standards, video AI can guarantee interoperability and compatibility with various applications and systems.
- **Help for Developers**: Enabling developers with all the tools and resources they need, such as documentation, SDKs, and APIs, helps hasten the creation and implementation of AI solutions.

## Transparent Innovation and Cooperation

Encouraging open innovation and teamwork can propel video AI forward and broaden its uses.

- **Research Collaborations:** Collaborating with educational establishments and research groups can result in advancements in artificial intelligence technologies and their utilization in the processing of videos.

- **Crowdsourcing:** By utilizing crowdsourcing platforms, a wide range of developers and academics can contribute their unique perspectives and creative ideas.

- **Open Source initiatives:** By fostering a robust community of contributors and accelerating innovation, open source AI initiatives can advance technology.

## 5.4: Finance and Investing

## Implications of AI Development for Finance

There are major financial ramifications to investing in AI development, both in terms of expenses and possible profits.

- **R&D Investment:** To advance AI technology and keep a competitive edge, significant investment in research and development is necessary.

- **Infrastructure Costs:** There are considerable expenses associated with creating and managing the high-performance computer resources and data storage needed for AI.

- **Long-term ROI:** Income from AI-powered goods and services can generate a sizable long-term return on investment, even with a hefty initial outlay.

## NVIDIA's Return on Investment

With numerous revenue streams, NVIDIA may see a significant return on investment from video AI.

- **Product Sales:** Sales of software and products that are AI-powered have the potential to be very profitable.

- **Service Subscriptions:** Making AI services available via a subscription model can generate a consistent flow of income.

- **Licensing Fees:** Granting licenses for AI

technologies to other businesses might result in recurring income and promote industry-wide uptake.

## Attracting Venture Capital and Investors

Getting venture capital and investors is essential for funding the advancement and growth of AI.

- **Investor Confidence:** Showing the market potential and video AI's capacity for generating income will bolster investor confidence and draw sizable investment.
- **Strategic Funding:** The funds required to grow AI development and commercialization can be obtained by securing strategic funding from venture capitalists and industry leaders.
- **Public Offerings:** Taking into account public offerings together with other capital-raising techniques can help secure extra cash for sustained expansion and innovation.

Video AI offers a wide range of business prospects and a significant economic impact. Companies such as NVIDIA can propel notable scientific improvements and economic growth in the video AI area by securing investment and funding, resolving industry disruptions, creating partnerships and collaborations, and investigating market potential.

# CHAPTER 6

## Consequences for Society and Culture

## 6.1: Effect on Art and Creativity

### Artists & Creators: AI as a Tool

With new tools and techniques to boost creativity, artificial intelligence (AI) technology is completely changing how artists and creators approach their work.

- **Enhanced Creativity:** AI-driven tools can help artists experiment with new styles and techniques, come up with fresh ideas, and automate tedious activities. Increased creative options and more effective workflows may result from this.
- **Working together with AI:** AI systems and artists can work together to create original works that combine human creativity with mechanical precision. This partnership may produce avant-garde

artistic creations and experiences.

- **Accessibility:** AI tools have the potential to democratize the use of advanced creative technology, enabling a wider spectrum of people, regardless of technical proficiency, to express themselves artistically.

## Applications for Novel Artistic Expressions

AI has the ability to open up hitherto unthinkable avenues for artistic expression.

- **Generative Art:** AI algorithms are capable of producing art on their own, producing works that are frequently unexpected and original. Visual art, music, literature, and even interactive installations fall under this category.
- **Interactive Art:** AI can help create interactive art experiences that react in real-time to input from viewers, making them more immersive and engaging.
- **Composite Media:** AI is capable of fluidly fusing different media types together, for example, visual

art and music or text, to produce complex artistic expressions.

## Considerations of Ethics in AI-Generated Art

A number of ethical issues are raised by the popularity of AI-generated art.

- **Authorship:** Since both the AI system and the human creator are involved, identifying the author and owner of works produced by AI can be difficult.
- **Value and Authenticity:** There may be debates over the authenticity and value of AI-generated art, especially in light of the emotional and intellectual components that are typically connected to human creativity.
- **influence on Jobs:** AI's ability to automate creative jobs may have an influence on artists' and creatives' employment prospects, requiring conversations on AI's place in the creative sector.

## 6.2: Shifts in Media Usage

## Customized Visual Experiences

AI is revolutionizing the way people consume media by making highly customized video experiences possible.

- **Content Recommendations:** Artificial intelligence algorithms examine viewer preferences and behavior to make personalized content recommendations that raise user satisfaction and engagement.
- **Customized Viewing:** Depending on their tastes, viewers can receive customized versions of content, such as rewritten sequences or different endings.
- **Dynamic Advertising:** AI makes it possible for targeted advertising to correspond with the interests of specific viewers, increasing the relevance and potency of advertisements.

## Engaging and Immersive Narration

Novel forms of immersive and interactive storytelling are

being promoted by the use of AI into media.

- **Interactive Narratives:** AI is able to produce branching stories that change based on decisions made by the spectator, providing a unique and captivating storytelling experience.
- **Augmented Reality (AR) and Virtual Reality (VR):** AI improves VR and AR experiences by building lifelike settings and interactions that draw viewers into the narrative.
- **Real-time Adaptation:** AI may instantly alter material in response to audience input and involvement, adding dynamic and responsiveness to the storytelling experience.

**Impact on Media Habits and Attention Span**

Media habits and attention span may be significantly impacted by AI-driven media consumption.

- **Short-form material:** Quick satisfaction and shorter attention spans are catered to by the growing popularity of AI-generated short-form material, such

TikTok videos.

- **Binge-Watching:** AI suggestions may promote binge-watching, which may have an adverse effect on the lifestyle and general well-being of viewers.

- **Content Overload:** The deluge of tailored content could result in content overload, which would make it difficult for consumers to efficiently control how much information they consume.

## 6.3: Social Media and Influencer Culture

**Social Media Content Creation Driven by AI**

Online relationships are changing as a result of the growing usage of AI in content creation for social media platforms.

- **Automated Content Creation:** Influencers and companies can keep a continuous online presence by using AI tools to create social media posts, videos, and photographs.

- **Content Optimization:** AI may enhance the reach and engagement of content by tailoring it to various audiences and platforms.

- **Virtual Influencers:** Artificial intelligence (AI) can produce virtual influencers, which are computer-generated personas that engage with followers and advertise brands.

## Reliability and Credibility of Online Content

Authenticity and trust are called into doubt by the employment of AI in content creation.

- **Transparency:** In order to preserve transparency and audience trust, content providers must reveal the usage of AI in content generation.
- **Authenticity:** Artificial intelligence-generated content's authenticity could come under scrutiny, especially if it lacks the human touch and emotional nuance of content produced by humans.
- **Trust Issues:** Deepfakes and other misleading or deceptive content that AI can produce have the potential to destroy public confidence in online media.

## Chance for Misinformation and Deepfakes

The potential of AI to produce lifelike deepfakes presents serious obstacles to the fight against misinformation.

- **Deepfake Risks:**Through malevolent use, deepfakes can propagate misinformation, sway public opinion, and damage reputations.
- **Detection and Mitigation:** Preserving the authenticity of online content requires the development of AI technologies for the detection and mitigation of deepfakes.
- **Regulatory Measures:** To address the moral and legal ramifications of deepfakes, governments and platforms must set rules and regulations.

## 6.4: Training and Education

### Digital Skills and AI Literacy

The increasing prevalence of AI demands that people of all demographics acquire digital skills and AI literacy.

- **Curriculum Integration:** To prepare students for the future labor market, educational institutions should incorporate digital literacy and artificial intelligence into their curricula.

- **Professional Development:** Employees should have access to chances for ongoing professional development so they can retrain and upskill in AI technology.

- **Public Awareness:** Initiatives to increase public knowledge of AI, its potential, and its social ramifications should be undertaken.

## Training Personnel for the AI Era

Several important tactics are needed to get the workforce ready for the AI age.

- **Skill Development:** Training curricula ought to concentrate on fostering the development of AI-related abilities, including machine learning, data science, and AI ethics.

- **Industrial Partnerships:** Working together, academic institutions and business can guarantee that training curricula reflect current technical developments and market demands.

- **lifetime Learning:** To assist workers in adjusting to the quickly evolving technology landscape, it is imperative to foster a culture of lifetime learning.

## AI and Ethical Education for Good

To guarantee that AI technologies are created and used properly, ethical education is essential.

- **Ethical Frameworks:** AI can be responsibly used in a variety of applications by developing and supporting ethical frameworks for the technology.
- **AI for Social Good:** Promoting the application of AI for social good, such as enhancing environmental sustainability, healthcare, and education, can highlight the benefits of this technology.
- **Public Engagement:** Including the public in conversations regarding AI ethics and how it affects society can help to increase trust as well as promote a more responsible and knowledgeable AI development process.

Artificial intelligence in video material has wide-ranging and significant societal and cultural ramifications. We can responsibly and thoughtfully handle the benefits and problems given by AI by being aware of the effects on creativity and art, changes in media consumption, the dynamics of social media and influencer culture, the value of education, and ethical considerations.

# CHAPTER 7

## THE GEOPOLITICAL LANDSCAPE AND GLOBAL COMPETITION

### 7.1: The Arms Race in AI

### Tech Giants in Competition

The fierce rivalry between large tech companies vying to be at the forefront of AI innovation is what defines the AI arms race.

- **Key Participants:** Leading companies in AI research and development, like Google, Amazon, Microsoft, and NVIDIA, are making significant investments in the field to obtain a competitive advantage.
- **AI Investment:** These massive IT companies are investing billions of dollars on artificial intelligence (AI), concentrating on advances in computer vision, natural language processing, and machine learning.

- **Acquiring Talent:** A vital component of this battle is luring top talent, with businesses providing attractive incentives to AI developers and researchers.

## Investment and Support from the Government in AI

Government engagement is essential in determining the global AI environment, as many countries have made AI development a top priority.

- **National AI Strategies:** Nations with a focus on research, funding, and implementation, such as the United States, China, and the European Union, have detailed comprehensive AI strategies.
- **Public-Private Partnerships:** Working together, public and private sector organizations expedite the development and application of AI while guaranteeing that resources and expertise are used efficiently.
- **Funding and Grants:** Governments encourage AI activities in academia and industry by offering grants and subsidies.

## Leadership in AI Technology Worldwide

Global leadership and economic power are significantly impacted by the competition for AI supremacy.

- **Technological Dominance:** Being at the forefront of AI technology can contribute to increased national security, better public services, and economic prosperity.
- **Influence on Standards:** Nations that lead the world in AI technology frequently establish international norms and standards, affecting AI laws and policies around the world.
- **Strategic Advantages:** Advanced AI capabilities allow nations to gain an advantage in a number of industries, such as banking, healthcare, and defense.

## 7.2: Trade and Intellectual Property Conflicts

## Protection of Data and AI Technology

One of the most important concerns in the global AI

environment is the protection of AI technology and related data.

- **Intellectual Property (IP) Rights:** Promoting ongoing research and development depends on providing strong IP protection for AI discoveries and technologies.
- **Data Privacy:** Since AI systems frequently need enormous volumes of personal data for operation and training, protecting data privacy is crucial.
- **Cybersecurity:** Preserving the security and trustworthiness of AI applications requires protecting AI systems and data from cyber attacks.

## Global Collaboration and Guidelines

Establishing universal guidelines and rules for AI technology requires international cooperation.

- **Standardization Efforts:** Global AI standards are being developed by organizations like the Institute of Electrical and Electronics Engineers (IEEE) and the International Organization for Standardization (ISO).

- **Cross-Border Collaboration:** Working together, nations may create standardized AI policies that guarantee safety and interoperability.

- **Sharing Best Practices:** Information and best practices exchanged among nations facilitate the adoption of successful AI legislation.

## Tensions in Geopolitics and the Development of AI

International relations are impacted by geopolitical issues that affect AI development and application.

- **Trade Disputes:** The availability of hardware and software components is impacted by trade conflicts that affect the global AI supply chain, such as those between the US and China.

- **Sanctions and Export Controls:** To safeguard national interests and keep enemies from obtaining access, governments may apply sanctions or export controls on AI technologies.

- **Diplomatic Relations**: Partnerships and alliances shape the global AI environment, and diplomatic relations play a function in AI collaboration.

## 7.3: Distinctions Between Ethics and Regulations

## International Differences in AI Ethics

Countries' approaches to AI ethics vary greatly from one another, reflecting different political, social, and cultural norms.

- **Ethical Frameworks:** Nations create their own AI-related ethical frameworks that handle matters like responsibility, transparency, and bias.
- **Human Rights Considerations:** Certain countries place a higher value on individual liberties and privacy than others, so it is important to make sure AI systems respect human rights.
- **Cultural Context:** Diverse viewpoints on what defines ethical AI result from the influence of cultural context on ethical considerations.

## Regulations on AI Harmonization

Although there are many obstacles along the way,

international efforts to unify AI legislation are crucial to guaranteeing the safe and efficient use of AI.

- **Regulatory Alignment:** Cooperation in AI technology and international trade can be facilitated by harmonizing rules among nations.
- **Compliance and Enforcement:** Strong enforcement tools and collaboration between regulatory agencies are necessary to guarantee adherence to global regulations.
- **Dynamic Regulation:** AI laws must be flexible in order to keep up with the quick speed at which technology is developing and the changing demands of society.

## International Collaboration's Challenges

There are various obstacles to international cooperation in AI development and regulation.

- **Divergent Interests:** It may be difficult to come to an agreement on AI policy due to different national priorities and interests.

- **Trust and Transparency:** Effective international partnerships depend on fostering trust and maintaining transparency.

- **Resource Disparities:** Differences in national capacities and resources can obstruct fair cooperation and information exchange.

## 7.4: National Security and AI

## Applications of AI in Security and Defense

Artificial Intelligence (AI) is revolutionizing military operations and intelligence with its vast applications in defense and national security.

- **Autonomous Systems:** AI-driven autonomous systems, such robotic cars and drones, improve military prowess and operational effectiveness.

- **Intelligence Analysis:** AI is capable of analyzing enormous volumes of data to find patterns and insights that guide strategic choices.

- **Cybersecurity:** AI strengthens cybersecurity by immediately identifying and addressing attacks, safeguarding vital infrastructure and national resources.

## Combining Technology and Export Regulations

AI technologies frequently have the potential to be used for both military and civilian applications.

- **Export Controls:** Nations impose export controls to manage the flow of AI technologies that enemies might use for military gains.
- **Balancing Innovation and Security:** To ensure that safety is not jeopardized by AI developments, it is imperative to strike a balance between the necessity for innovation and concerns about national security.
- **International Agreements:** Treaties and agreements at the international level seek to regulate the spread of dual-use technology while encouraging ethical AI development.

## Synergizing Innovation with Homeland Security

It is a difficult task to strike a balance between national

security concerns and the desire for AI advancement.

- **Innovation Incentives:** Establishing a conducive research and development environment, including resources, infrastructure, and personnel development, is essential to fostering innovation in artificial intelligence.
- **Security Measures:** AI technology is safeguarded against abuse and cyber risks by putting strong security measures in place.
- **Policy and Regulation:** Creating thorough rules and guidelines that take into account security and innovation requirements is crucial for the long-term development of artificial intelligence.

The development and application of AI technologies are greatly influenced by the geopolitical environment and global rivalry. Stakeholders can effectively manage the complex dynamics of the AI era by grasping the AI arms race, intellectual property and trade disputes, ethical and regulatory issues, and the consequences for national security.

# CHAPTER 8

## NVIDIA's Opportunities and Challenges

### 8.1: Technical Difficulties

### Overcoming Current AI Model Limitations

Even with these tremendous advances, there are still a number of technical issues with present AI models that must be resolved for them to operate to their fullest capacity.

- **Scalability:** Scaling artificial intelligence algorithms to effectively handle enormous volumes of data is one of the main issues. Models need to be able to process and learn from more data without experiencing a decrease in performance as the number of data increases.

- **Oversimplification:** It is imperative to guarantee that AI models exhibit strong cross-domain and task generalization. When applied to new circumstances, current models frequently require significant retraining because of their poor transfer learning capabilities.

- **Efficiency of Energy:** Deep learning networks in particular, which are AI models, require a lot of processing power, which drives up energy expenses. The development of more energy-efficient hardware and algorithms is necessary for the deployment of AI sustainably.

## Maintaining Robustness and Reliability in AI Systems

For AI systems to be used in real-world scenarios where mistakes might have serious repercussions, they must be robust and reliable.

- **Error Rates:** It is critical to lower the error rates in AI predictions. Strict testing and validation are required in order to detect and minimize possible points of failure.
- **Attack Resistance against Adversaries:** Artificial intelligence (AI) systems need to be resilient to

adversarial assaults that alter inputs to generate false results. One important area of research is creating defenses against these kinds of attacks.

- **Stability in Operations:** Reliability of AI systems depends on ensuring that they perform consistently under a range of workloads and environments. This involves successfully handling edge circumstances and unexpected inputs.

## Taking Fairness and Biases in AI

To guarantee moral and just results, bias and fairness in AI are important issues that must be resolved.

- **Identifying and Reducing Biases:** To avoid biased results, biases in AI models must be found and mitigated. This entails creating methods for identifying bias and putting fairness constraints in place while the model is being trained.

- **Comprehensive Datasets:** Biases are lessened when AI models are trained on a variety of representative datasets. It is imperative for fairness that these databases encompass a range of demographics and scenarios.

- **Accountability and Transparency:** Establishing accountability and transparency in AI systems contributes to the development of trust. This entails letting humans supervise and intervene as well as explaining AI judgments.

## 8.2: Difficulties in Business

## Revenue Streams and Monetization Techniques

NVIDIA must successfully commercialize its AI advancements in order to create long-term income sources.

- **Product Differentiation:** In order to draw clients and get higher prices in a cutthroat industry, AI goods and services must stand out from the competition.
- **Models of Subscription:** By using subscription models, AI solutions can generate recurring income and increase client loyalty. Strong customer service and service delivery are necessary for this strategy.
- Collaborations and Grants: Creating strategic

alliances and licensing contracts with other businesses can help you reach a wider audience and generate more income.

## Market Share and Competition

For NVIDIA, keeping a competitive edge in the quickly changing AI market is a major issue.

- **Competitive Landscape:** There are many IT giants and startups fighting for dominance in the fiercely competitive AI field. To stay ahead, NVIDIA needs to innovate constantly.
- **Sector Infiltration:** Effective marketing, sales tactics, and local relationships are necessary to increase market penetration in both existing and new territories.
- **Switching with the Times:** Agile development and the capacity to swiftly modify AI services to changing needs are essential for staying up to date with industry trends and client wants.

# Preserving an Advantage in AI

In order to maintain its leadership in AI, NVIDIA needs to keep improving both its product portfolio and market standing.

- **Information and Development:** Research and development (R&D) spending is essential to preserving technical leadership. Investigating state-of-the-art AI methods and applications is part of this.
- **Talent Acquisition:** Innovation cannot be advanced without attracting and keeping the best AI talent. Retaining important workers is facilitated by offering an engaging work environment and chances for professional development.
- **Customer Focus:** By identifying and meeting the needs of each individual customer, as well as providing outstanding service, enduring connections and brand loyalty are fostered.

## 8.3: Room for Development

## Growing in New Verticals and Markets

NVIDIA has a lot of potential to grow its AI portfolio by entering new industries and business sectors.

- **Healthcare:** There are significant growth prospects for AI applications in the healthcare industry, such as medical imaging and diagnostics. NVIDIA's proficiency in GPU technology can propel progress in this field.

- **Engine:** AI is being used more and more in the automobile sector for advanced driver assistance systems (ADAS) and autonomous driving. The AI products from NVIDIA may be essential to this change.

- **Finance:** AI-powered fraud detection and analytics present new business prospects for the banking industry. NVIDIA can offer predictive analytics and risk management solutions by utilizing its AI capabilities.

## Using AI to Enhance Other NVIDIA Products

NVIDIA's current product line can be made more functional and valuable for customers by using AI.

- **Graphics and Gaming:** AI has the power to provide more realistic graphics, boost game performance, and produce more immersive gaming environments. These apps already make extensive use of NVIDIA's GPUs.

- **Data Centers:** AI can streamline operations in data centers, increasing productivity and cutting expenses. Data center management systems can be connected with NVIDIA's AI technologies.

- **Edge Computing:** AI at the edge allows IoT devices to process and make decisions in real-time. NVIDIA is able to create AI programs specifically for edge computing uses.

## Developing New Business Frameworks

Novel business models have the potential to propel

NVIDIA's expansion and create fresh sources of income.

- **AI-as-a-Service (AIaaS):** By providing cloud-based services with AI capabilities, clients can access and use AI solutions without having to make substantial upfront investments.

- **Custom AI Solutions:** NVIDIA can stand out from the competition and draw in specialized markets by offering AI solutions that are specifically designed to meet industry needs.

- **Development of the AI Ecosystem:** Creating a strong AI ecosystem via collaborations and developer assistance encourages creativity and generates a network effect, which accelerates the uptake of NVIDIA's AI technologies.

## 8.4: Mitigation and Risk Management

**Determining Possible Dangers and Hazards**

To ensure the security of NVIDIA's AI activities, it is imperative to proactively identify and mitigate possible vulnerabilities.

- **Technical Risks:** AI implementations are susceptible to technical difficulties like scalability problems and system vulnerabilities. It takes constant observation and development to reduce these dangers.

- **Market Hazards:** AI product success may be impacted by shifting consumer tastes and market instability. It is essential to comprehend market dynamics and modify strategy as necessary.

- **Perils of Regulation:** AI development and implementation may be impacted by changing compliance standards and regulatory environments. It's crucial to stay up to date on regulatory developments and make sure compliance.

## Creating Backup Strategies

Business continuity may be ensured by putting contingency planning in place to prepare for possible disruptions.

- **Crisis Management:** Making strategies for crisis management in case of data breaches or system failures guarantees quick and efficient reactions.

- **Redundancy and Backup:** By putting in place redundancy and backup systems, you can reduce data loss and downtime in the event of technological malfunctions.

- **Evaluation of Risk**: Risk assessments should be carried out on a regular basis to assist identify vulnerabilities and prioritize mitigation measures.

## Developing Adaptability and Resilience

Long-term success in a changing environment is ensured by including resilience and adaptation into AI strategy.

- **Agile Development:** Using agile development approaches enables quick iteration and adjustment to shifting specifications and market dynamics.

- **Continuous Learning:** Encouraging a culture of ongoing learning and development enables NVIDIA to meet new challenges head-on and remain at the forefront of AI innovation.

- **Involvement of Stakeholders:** Including customers, partners, and regulators in the process guarantees that AI projects are in line with more general industry trends and specifications.

NVIDIA has a lot of business and technical obstacles to overcome in the AI space, but there are also a lot of growth and innovation prospects. NVIDIA can maintain its position as a leader in AI technology by resolving technical issues, improving commercial plans, and effectively managing risks.

# CHAPTER 9

## AI's ROLE IN VIDEO CONTENT

### 9.1: Forecasts and Patterns

### Upcoming Advances in Video Artificial Intelligence

The field of video AI technology is developing quickly, and there are a number of significant trends and developments to look forward to:

- **Improved Quality and Realism:** It is anticipated that future advancements will push the limits of video realism. Through sophisticated upscaling methods, noise reduction, and more precise color reproduction, AI models will enhance image and video quality, producing hyper-realistic video material.

- **Automated Generation of Content:** AI will gradually automate the processes involved in creating content, from creating storyboards and video scripts to creating completely animated sequences. Workflows will be streamlined as a result, freeing up creators to concentrate on more complex creative projects.

- **Innovations in Deep Learning:** More complex effects and transformations will be possible thanks to developments in deep learning architectures like transformers and generative adversarial networks (GANs), which will improve video synthesis and manipulation capabilities.

## Impact on Production and Consumption of Content

The creation and consumption of video material will be profoundly impacted by the incorporation of AI:

- **Personalized Experiences:** AI will make it possible to create extremely customized video experiences by adjusting interactive components and content recommendations based on each viewer's unique interests and viewing behaviors. This will increase user engagement.

- **Efficiency in Production:** Artificial intelligence (AI)-powered tools will optimize video production procedures, saving money and time on post-production, special effects, and editing. This will make it easier for more people to create high-quality videos, democratizing the process of content creation.

- **Interactive and Immersive Formats:** New interactive and immersive video formats, such augmented reality (AR) and virtual reality (VR), will be supported by emerging AI technologies, resulting in more captivating and interactive viewing experiences.

## New Use Cases and Applications

In the video space, AI will open up a wide range of new use cases and applications:

- **Real-Time Translation and Subtitling:** Artificial intelligence will make it easier to translate and subtitle video content in real-time, removing linguistic boundaries and opening up content to a worldwide audience.

- **AI-Driven Storytelling:** Cutting-edge AI tools will make dynamic storytelling approaches possible. In these techniques, the story changes in response to viewer choices or interactions, resulting in individualized and engaging experiences.

- **Advanced Video Analysis:** Artificial intelligence (AI) will improve video analysis features including scene recognition, emotion detection, and behavioral analysis. These features can be used in marketing, security, and entertainment, among other domains.

## 9.2: Consequences for Society

### Responsible AI and Ethical Issues

With the increasing integration of AI into video material, ethical considerations will become increasingly important.

- **Authenticity of Content:** Verifying the legitimacy of artificial intelligence-generated content is essential to avoiding manipulation and false information. Real and synthetic media will need to be distinguished from one another by obvious labeling and verification procedures.

- **Inequality and Bias: I**t is imperative to tackle biases in AI algorithms in order to avert discriminatory consequences and guarantee equitable representation of video material. Training models on a variety of representative datasets requires work.

- **Protective Issues:** Concerns about privacy are raised by the use of AI in video material, especially when it comes to data collecting and surveillance. Responsible AI implementation requires establishing strong privacy policies and obtaining user consent.

**Accessibility and the Digital Divide**

The digital gap and accessibility must be addressed by AI developments in video content:

- **Equitable Access:** To close the digital gap and advance inclusivity, it is imperative that AI-driven video technology be available to everyone, irrespective of location or socioeconomic background.

- **Support for Diverse demands:** AI systems ought to be made to take into account a range of demands, including those of people with disabilities. This entails putting in place functions like audio descriptions and automated captioning.

- **Education and Training:** By assisting people and communities in making the most of AI technology, education and training may promote increased digital literacy and empowerment.

## Human-AI Cooperation and Enhancement

The production of video content in the future will progressively require human and AI collaboration:

- **Augmented Creativity:** By offering resources and perspectives that improve the creative process, AI will supplement human creativity. AI will be used by filmmakers, artists, and content producers to explore new creative ideas and produce inventive results.

- **Collaborative Workflows:** AI will support cooperative workflows in which the skills of humans and AI are complementary. Productivity will increase as a result, opening the door to more ambitious and sophisticated initiatives.

- **Skill Development:** AI will help with skill development and training by giving those studying video creation, editing, and other relevant skills real-time feedback and support.

## 9.3: NVIDIA's Function

### Creating the Video Content of the Future

With its AI technologies, NVIDIA is well-positioned to influence the direction of video content in the future:

- **Innovative Solutions:** NVIDIA's breakthroughs in AI models and GPU technology will spur creativity in the production, editing, and analysis of video material, establishing new benchmarks for functionality and quality.
- **Industrial Leadership:** NVIDIA will impact best practices and industry trends as a pioneer in AI technology, assisting in the creation of innovative

video solutions and applications.

- **Strategic Partnerships**: NVIDIA will be able to incorporate its AI solutions into a variety of video applications and platforms through partnerships with content creators, studios, and technology businesses.

## Innovation in AI Leadership

The video industry and other sectors will be impacted by NVIDIA's leadership in AI innovation:

- **Research and Development**: NVIDIA's R&D spending will keep pushing the limits of AI technology, bringing forth fresh discoveries and improvements that will help the video content industry.
- **Thought Leadership**: NVIDIA will influence conversations about the future of artificial intelligence in video and encourage the proper use of AI technology through industry conferences, publications, and partnerships.
- **Technology Ecosystem**: By creating tools, platforms, and frameworks that encourage the

expansion and uptake of AI in the production and distribution of video content, NVIDIA will contribute to the larger AI ecosystem.

## Effect on the World Technology Scene

NVIDIA has an impact on the worldwide tech environment in addition to the video industry:

- **Driving Innovation:** By offering cutting-edge capabilities and solutions, NVIDIA's AI technologies will spur innovation in a number of industries, including healthcare, automotive, and finance.
- **Global Competitiveness:** NVIDIA will be more competitive globally thanks to its leadership in AI, which will establish the business as a major player in the technology industry and have an impact on global tech trends.
- **Economic Growth:** By promoting technical development, opening up new business opportunities, and creating jobs, NVIDIA's inventions and advancements will help the economy

expand.

## 9.4: A Prospective View

## AI's Possible Benefits to Society

Artificial intelligence (AI) has the potential to significantly improve society through its use in video content and other fields.

- **Enhanced Communication:** Artificial intelligence (AI)-powered video technology can boost connectivity and communication, enabling distant interactions and teamwork in a range of settings, including business, healthcare, and education.
- **Increased Creativity:** AI will enable people and organizations to experiment with new kinds of artistic expression and creativity by giving them access to strong tools for content generation and manipulation.
- **Improved Accessibility:** With features like automatic captioning, translations, and assistive technology, AI can make video content more

accessible to a wider range of audiences, including people with impairments.

## Overcoming Obstacles and Reducing Dangers

In order to fully utilize AI, the following risks and problems need to be addressed:

- **Regulatory Frameworks:** Establishing and putting into place efficient regulatory frameworks will guarantee the appropriate application of AI technologies while safeguarding the privacy and rights of users.
- **Ethical Standards:** Fairness, accountability, and transparency in AI systems will be enhanced by the establishment of ethical standards and guidelines for AI development and deployment.
- **Public Awareness:** Educating the public about the advantages and disadvantages of artificial intelligence (AI) will encourage thoughtful debates and choices, resulting in more responsible and advantageous AI applications.

# Using AI to Create a Positive Future

AI requires proactive efforts and teamwork to build a positive future:

- **Collaborative Efforts:** The development of AI technologies that are in line with societal ideals and needs will be fueled by cooperation between technology corporations, legislators, educators, and the general public.
- **Continuous Improvement:** Ongoing research and development will guarantee that AI technologies keep improving and changing, tackling new problems and boosting their beneficial effects.
- **Shared Vision:** The responsible development and application of AI technologies will be guided by a shared vision for the future of AI that places an emphasis on innovation, ethical issues, and social advantages.

There is a lot of promise for video content and artificial intelligence in the future. New developments in technology can lead to revolutionary new avenues for accessibility, creativity, and communication. Through tackling obstacles and adopting a cooperative methodology, interested parties can mold a constructive and all-encompassing AI future.

# CHAPTER 10

## 10.1: Key Findings Synopsis

## NVIDIA's Video AI Initiative Recap

An important step forward in the artificial intelligence and video technology integration process is represented by NVIDIA's video AI program. In order to improve video production, editing, and analysis, the company has released cutting-edge AI models and tools. Important components of this endeavor consist of:

- **Creative AI Models:** NVIDIA has created cutting-edge AI models that push the limits of video quality, interaction, and realism. These models produce and modify video content with previously unheard-of accuracy by utilizing deep learning, computer vision, and natural language processing.

- **Impact on Market:** Thanks to its innovations, NVIDIA is now a market leader in video AI, impacting practices and standards within the industry. The technology of the company has the potential to revolutionize workflows in video production and improve the viewing experience for consumers.

- **Strategic Vision:** NVIDIA's strategy blends collaborations with technological innovation to help define the future of video content and propel the creation of new applications and use cases.

## Effect on Diverse Parties

NVIDIA's video AI program has an impact on a number of stakeholders:

- **Content Creators:** AI-driven technologies improve creative potential, expedite production processes, and cut expenses for creators. These tools create new avenues for artistic expression and facilitate more productive processes.

- **Customers:** AI-enhanced video content provides

consumers with unique formats, better quality, and personalized experiences. Their pleasure and engagement with the information they consume are improved by this customisation.

- **Industry Players:** NVIDIA's innovations have an impact on media companies, advertising agencies, and technology suppliers. The company's innovations spur competition, establish new benchmarks, and provide doors for cooperation and expansion.

## Potential Advantages and Difficulties

There are advantages and disadvantages to integrating AI into video content:

## Advantages:

1. **Enhanced Productivity:** AI may automate labor-intensive jobs, increasing output and cutting expenses.

2. **Enhanced Creativity:** New avenues for content creation are opened up by the use of sophisticated and imaginative video effects made possible by

advanced AI capabilities.

3. **Personalization:** AI enables engaging experiences and personalized content recommendations, increasing viewer pleasure.

## Difficulties:

1. **Ethical Issues**: Concerns of potential biases, privacy, and authenticity of content are raised by the usage of AI. Ensuring appropriate usage is essential.

2. **Technical Limitations:** Despite improvements, accuracy and dependability of AI models are still limited, necessitating continued study and development.

3. **Areas of Regulation:** As regulations change, it becomes more difficult to maintain compliance and deal with moral and legal concerns around AI and video content.

## 10.2: Suggestions

## NVIDIA Strategies

In order to optimize the effects of its video AI endeavor,

NVIDIA ought to take into account the subsequent tactics:

- **Ongoing Innovation:** Make investments in R&D to progress AI technology and resolve existing constraints. To sustain its competitive advantage, NVIDIA will continue to be at the forefront of innovation.
- **Strategic Partnerships**: Encourage partnerships to integrate AI solutions into a variety of platforms and applications with media businesses, content creators, and other technology providers.
- **Ethical Leadership:** Create and follow moral standards for AI development and use. Encouraging accountability and openness will reduce possible risks and foster stakeholder trust.

## Government Policy Recommendations

The regulatory landscape for AI is significantly shaped by governments. Among the suggested policies are:

- **Creating Explicit laws:** Formulate thorough and lucid laws that tackle the moral, legal, and private ramifications of artificial intelligence in video content. Innovation and business and individual protection should be balanced in these regulations.

- **Encouraging Transparency:** Demand disclosures regarding the use of AI in video material, including details on data sources, algorithms, and potential biases, in order to promote transparency in AI technologies.

- **Supporting Research and Education:** Make investments in projects that advance knowledge of artificial intelligence and its uses. This involves giving resources for the development of ethical AI, encouraging AI literacy, and sponsoring scholarly study.

## Recommendations for Business and Customers

It is advised that consumers and industry participants adhere to the following guidelines:

## For Industry:

- **Adopt Best Practices:** Adhere to best practices on security, privacy, and moral application of AI. This entails carrying out frequent audits and putting in place strong data protection procedures.

- **Collaborate and Share Knowledge:** Take part in industry-wide partnerships to tackle shared problems and exchange expertise regarding artificial intelligence technology and their uses.

**Attention to Customer**s:

- **Remain Updated:** Learn about artificial intelligence (AI) technologies and how they affect video content. Making educated decisions can be aided by knowing how AI influences recommendations and content development.

- **Speak Up for Openness**: Encourage initiatives aimed at bringing more accountability and transparency to AI technologies. Encourage the provision of information about AI-generated material and proper labeling.

## 10.3: Prospects for Further Research

**Fields Needing More Research**

To further the subject of video AI, future research should concentrate on three important areas:

- **Improving AI Models:** Research ought to focus on boosting the precision, dependability, and adaptability of AI models applied to video content. Creating new architectures and methods to overcome existing constraints is part of this.

- **Ethical and Social Implications:** Examine the moral and societal ramifications of artificial intelligence in video material, taking into account concerns about bias, privacy, and false information. The creation of frameworks to allay these worries is necessary for the proper application of AI.

- **Integration with Emerging Technologies:** Investigate how artificial intelligence (AI) can be combined with other cutting-edge technologies, such virtual reality (VR) and augmented reality (AR), to produce fresh and inventive audiovisual experiences.

**Open-ended queries and difficulties**

Future study must address the following issues and open

questions:

- **Privacy of Data:** How can AI technology be used to create video content while efficiently protecting data privacy? Which procedures work best to guarantee user consent and data protection?

- **Inequality and Bias:** How can artificial intelligence models be created to reduce biases and guarantee equity in video content? What tactics can be used to produce objective results?

- **Legal Structures:** Which legal structures work best to control artificial intelligence (AI) in video content? How can laws keep up with the quick development of technology?

## The Continual Development of Video and AI

The future of the video and artificial intelligence (AI) industries will be shaped by continuous developments in these fields.

- **Technological Advancements:** As AI continues to advance, new advances in video technology will follow, creating experiences that are more complex and immersive.

- **Adapting to Change:** As AI and video content continue to evolve, industry participants and consumers alike will need to adjust, embracing new technology and tackling new obstacles.

- **End-of-Term Effect:** The future of artificial intelligence (AI) in video content will be influenced by continuing research, moral issues, and stakeholders working together to maximize benefits and minimize risks.

## 10.4: Closing Remarks

## A Consideration on the Consequences of Video AI

Deep ramifications for creativity, industry processes, and social standards arise from the incorporation of AI into video output. Artificial Intelligence (AI) technologies have revolutionary prospects for content production, augmenting video experiences in terms of quality and accessibility. To guarantee responsible use, these developments do, however, also present moral and legal issues.

# A Call to Accountability in Development

All stakeholders, tech companies, regulators, business leaders, and consumers must collaborate to promote the responsible development and application of AI technologies as the field progresses. This comprises:

- **Encouraging Ethical Standards:** To guarantee equity, accountability, and transparency in AI development and use, ethical standards must be adopted and followed.
- **Enhancing Collaboration:** Promoting cooperation amongst stakeholders in order to tackle shared problems, exchange best practices, and responsibly spur innovation.
- **Supporting educated Decisions:** Promoting public understanding of AI technology and their ramifications as well as educated decision-making.

# A Positive Prognosis for the Future

AI and video content have a bright future ahead of them

that could improve accessibility, creativity, and communication. We can build a bright and inclusive future where artificial intelligence (AI) advances society and improves our digital experiences by embracing innovation and tackling its problems. AI is still evolving, which means there is still room for development and advancement. If we work together, we can create a future where this game-changing technology is fully utilized.

# ABOUT THE AUTHOR

 Author and thought leader in the IT field Taylor Royce is well known. He has a two-decade career and is an expert at tech trend analysis and forecasting, which enables a wide audience to understand complicated concepts.

Royce's considerable involvement in the IT industry stemmed from his passion with technology, which he developed during his computer science studies. He has extensive knowledge of the industry because of his experience in both software development and strategic consulting.

Known for his research and lucidity, he has written multiple best-selling books and contributed to esteemed tech periodicals. Translations of Royce's books throughout the world demonstrate his impact.

Royce is a well-known authority on emerging technologies and their effects on society, frequently requested as a speaker at international conferences and as a guest on tech podcasts. He promotes the development of ethical technology, emphasizing problems like data privacy and the digital divide.

In addition, with a focus on sustainable industry growth, Royce mentors upcoming tech experts and supports IT education projects. Taylor Royce is well known for his ability to combine analytical thinking with technical know-how. He sees a time when technology will ethically benefit humanity.